BOB DYLAN
FOR EASY PIANO

Cover photo: Jerry Schatzberg / Trunk Archive

EXCLUSIVELY DISTRIBUTED BY
Hal•Leonard®

Visit Hal Leonard Online at
www.halleonard.com

ALL ALONG THE WATCHTOWER

Words and Music by
BOB DYLAN

"There must be some way out ___ of here," ___ said the jok-er to the thief."

"There's too much ___ con-fu - sion, _____

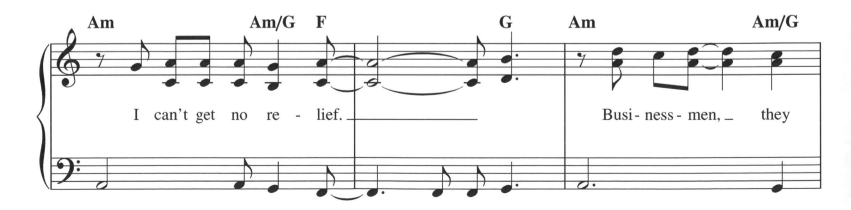

I can't get no re - lief. _____ Busi-ness-men, ___ they

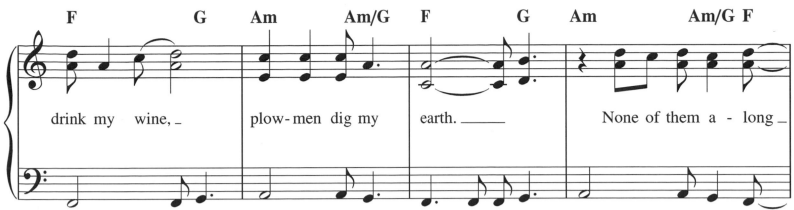

drink my wine, ____ plow-men dig my earth. ____ None of them a - long ____

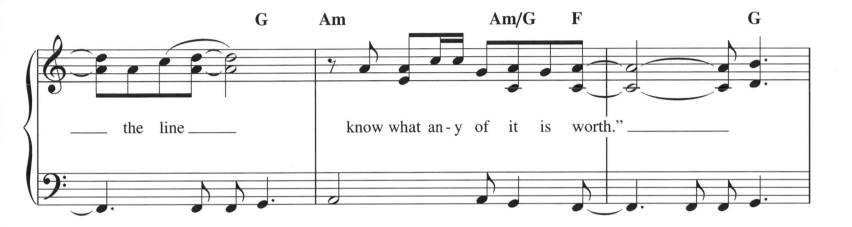

____ the line ____ know what an-y of it is worth." ____

"No rea-son to get ex-cit - ed," ____ the thief, he kind-ly spoke. ____

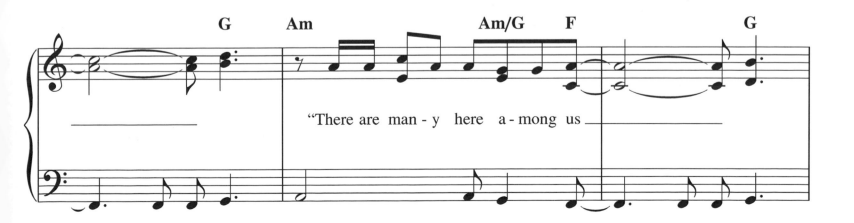

"There are man-y here a-mong us ____

who feel that life is but a joke. _____ But you and I, we've been _

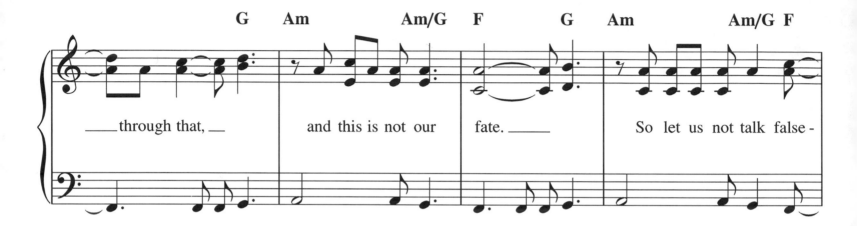

_ through that, _ and this is not our fate. _____ So let us not talk false-

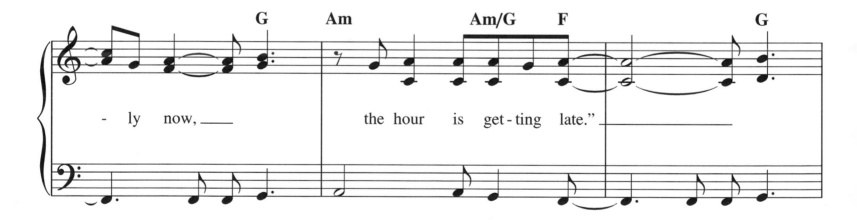

- ly now, ____ the hour is get-ting late." _____

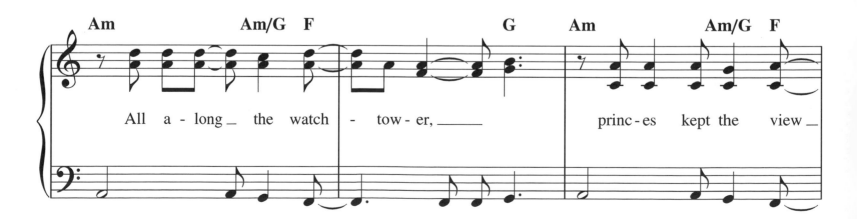

All a-long _ the watch - tow - er, _____ princ-es kept the view _

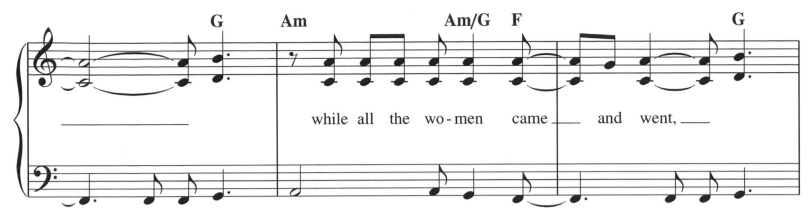

while all the wo-men came ___ and went, ___

bare-foot ser-vants, too. ___ Out-side in the dis - tance, ___

a wild-cat did growl. ___ Two rid-ers were ap-proach-

- ing, ___ the wind be-gan to howl. ___

poco rit.

BLOWIN' IN THE WIND

Words and Music by
BOB DYLAN

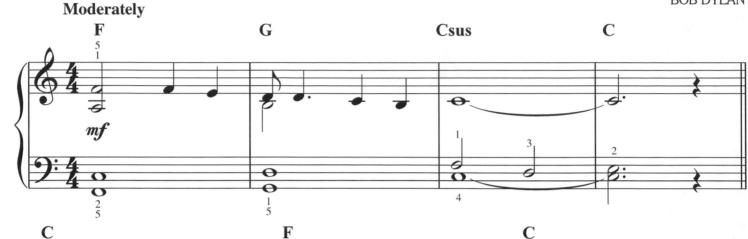

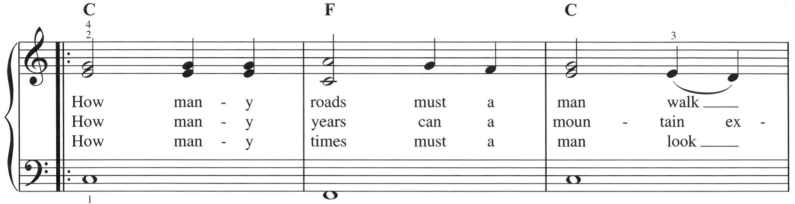

How | man - y | roads | must | a | man | walk ___
How | man - y | years | can | a | moun - tain | ex -
How | man - y | times | must | a | man | look ___

down | be - | fore | you | call | him | a
ist | be - | fore | it's | washed | to | the
up | be - | fore he | can | see | the ___

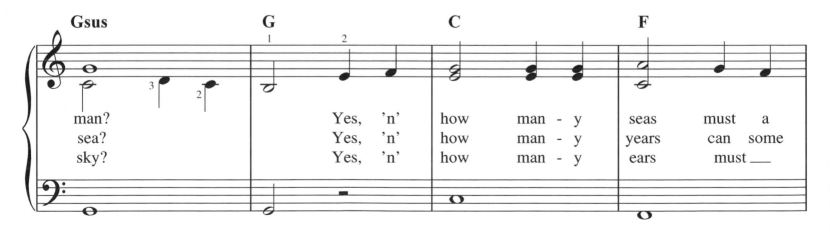

man? | | Yes, 'n' | how | man - y | seas | must | a
sea? | | Yes, 'n' | how | man - y | years | can | some
sky? | | Yes, 'n' | how | man - y | ears | must ___

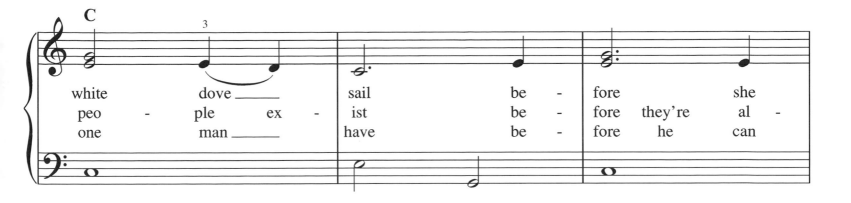

white dove ____ sail be - fore she
peo - ple ex - ist be - fore they're al -
one man ____ have be - fore he can

sleeps in the sand? ____ Yes, 'n' how man - y
lowed to be free? ____ Yes, 'n' how man - y
hear peo - ple cry? ____ Yes, 'n' how man - y

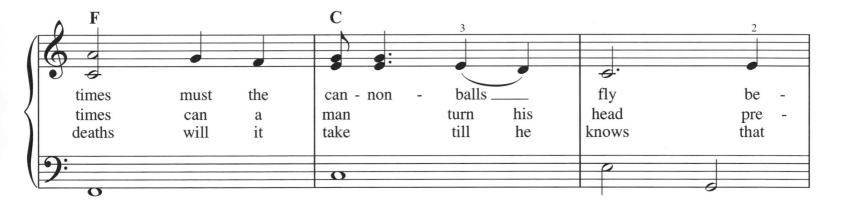

times must the can - non - balls ____ fly be -
times can a man turn his head pre -
deaths will it take till he knows that

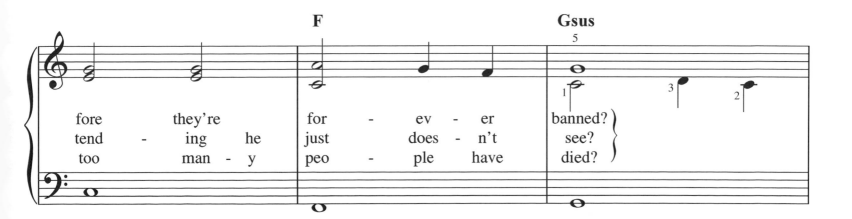

fore they're for - ev - er banned?
tend - ing he just does - n't see?
too man - y peo - ple have died?

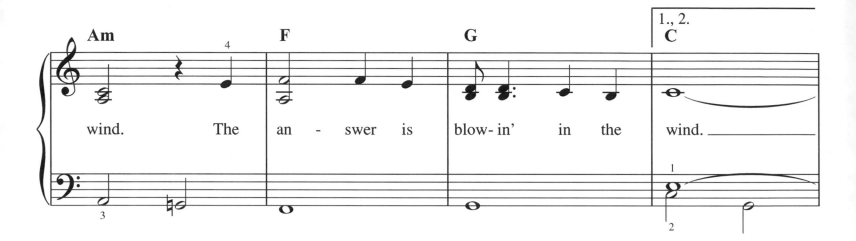

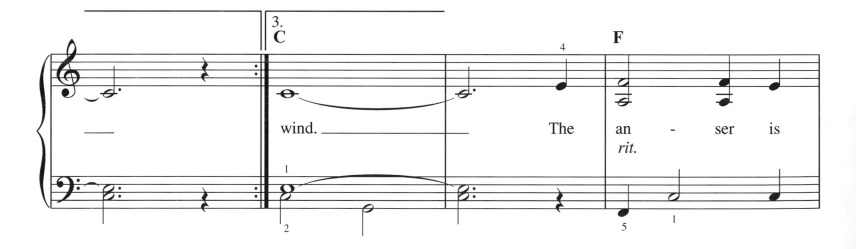

FOREVER YOUNG

Words and Music by
BOB DYLAN

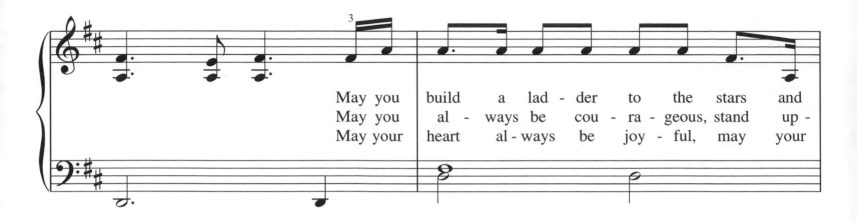

May you   build   a   lad - der   to   the   stars   and
May you   al - ways   be   cou - ra - geous, stand   up -
May your   heart   al - ways   be   joy - ful,   may   your

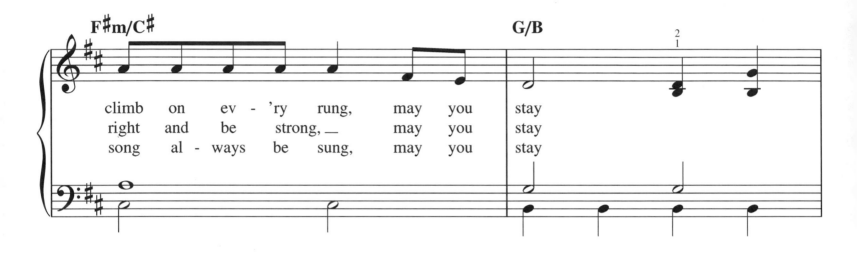

F#m/C#   **G/B**

climb   on   ev - 'ry   rung,   may   you   stay
right   and   be   strong, __   may   you   stay
song   al - ways   be   sung,   may   you   stay

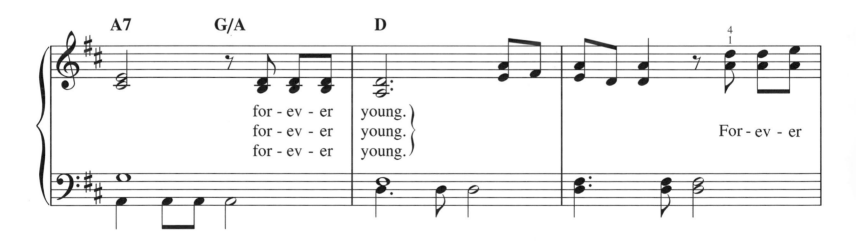

A7   **G/A**   **D**

for - ev - er   young.
for - ev - er   young.
for - ev - er   young.

For - ev - er

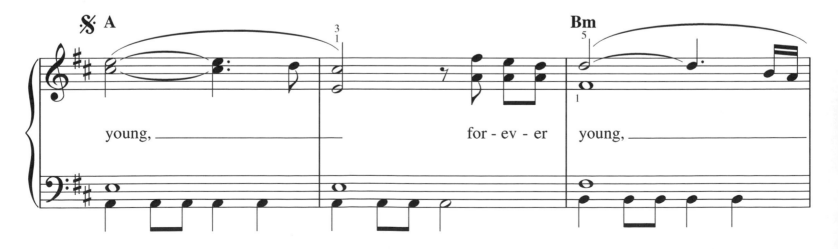

A   **Bm**

young, _____   for - ev - er   young, _____

HURRICANE

Words and Music by BOB DYLAN
and JACQUES LEVY

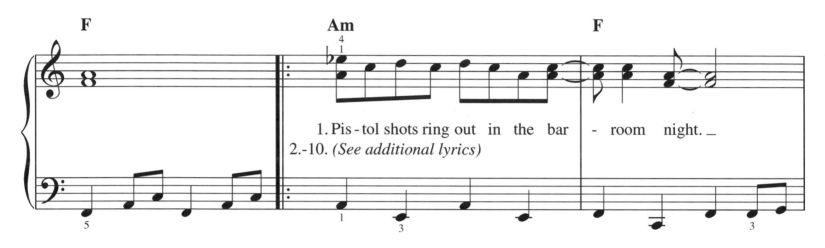

1. Pis-tol shots ring out in the bar - room night. __
2.-10. *(See additional lyrics)*

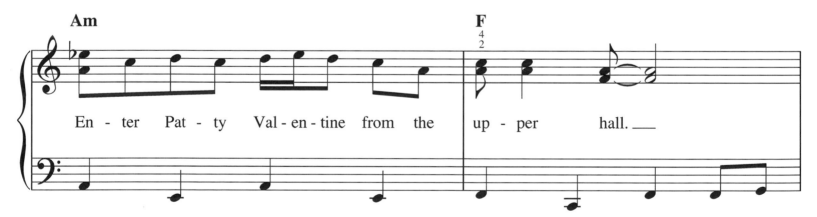

En - ter Pat-ty Val-en-tine from the up - per hall. __

She sees the bar-tend-er in a pool of blood. __

Cries out, "My God, they killed ____ them all!" Here comes the sto - ry of the

Hur - ri - cane, _ the man the au - thor - i - ties came ____ to blame _

for some-thin' that he nev - er done. Put in a pris-on cell, but

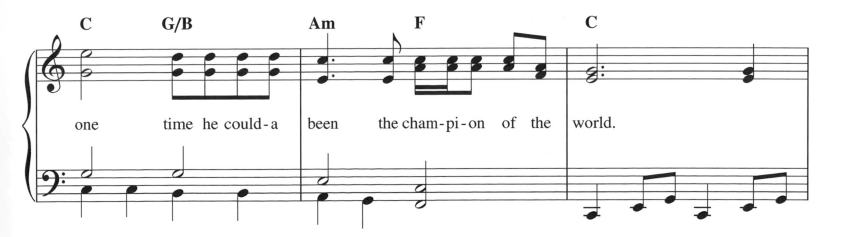

one time he could-a been the cham-pi - on of the world.

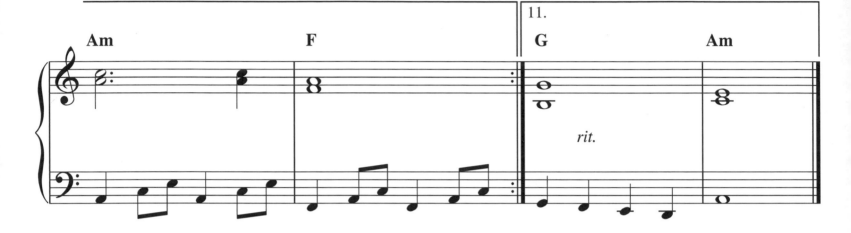

Additional Lyrics

2. Three bodies lyin' there does Patty see
   And another man named Bello, movin' around mysteriously
   "I didn't do it," he says, and throws up his hands
   "I was only robbin' the register, I hope you understand
   I saw them leavin'," he says, and he stops
   "One of us had better call up the cops"
   And so Patty calls the cops
   And they arrive on the scene with their red lights flashin'
   In the hot New Jersey night

3. Meanwhile, far away in another part of town
   Rubin Carter and a couple of friends are drivin' around
   Number one contender for the middleweight crown
   Had no idea what kinda shit was about to go down
   When a cop pulled him over to the side of the road
   Just like the time before and the time before that
   In Patterson that's just the way things go
   If you're black you might as well not show up on the street
   'Less you wanta draw the heat

4. Alfred Bello had a partner and he had a rap for the cops
   Him and Arthur Dexter Bradley were just out prowlin' around
   He said, "I saw two men runnin' out,
     they looked like middleweights
   They jumped into a white car with out-of-state plates"
   And Miss Patty Valentine just nodded her head
   Cop said, "Wait a minute boys, this one's not dead"
   So they took him to the infirmary
   And though this man could hardly see
   They told him that he could identify the guilty men

5. Four in the mornin' and they haul Rubin in
   Take him to the hospital and they bring him upstairs
   The wounded man looks up through his one dyin' eye
   Says, "Wha'd you bring him in here for? He ain't the guy!"
   Yes, here's the story of the Hurricane
   The man the authorities came to blame
   For somethin' that he never done
   Put in a prison cell, but one time he could-a been
   The champion of the world

6. Four months later, the ghettoes are in flame
   Rubin's in South America, fightin' for his name
   While Arthur Dexter Bradley's still in the robbery game
   And the cops are puttin' the screws to him, lookin' for somebody to blame
   "Remember that murder that happened in a bar?"
   "Remember you said you saw the getaway car?"
   "You think you'd like to play ball with the law?"
   "Think it might-a been that figher that you saw runnin' that night?"
   "Don't forget that you are white"

7. Arthur Dexter Bradley said, "I'm really not sure"
   Cops said, "A poor boy like you could use a break
   We got you for the motel job and we're talkin' to your friend Bello
   Now you don't wanta have to go back to jail, be a nice fellow
   You'll be doin' society a favor
   That sonofabitch is brave and gettin' braver
   We want to put his ass in stir
   We want to pin this triple murder on him
   He ain't no Gentleman Jim"

8. Rubin could take a man out with just one punch
   But he never did like to talk about it all that much
   It's my work, he'd say, and I do it for pay
   And when it's over I'd just as soon go on my way
   Up to some paradise
   Where the trout streams flow and the air is nice
   And ride a horse along a trail
   But then they took him to the jailhouse
   Where they try to turn a man into a mouse

9. All of Rubin's cards were marked in advance
   The trial was a pig-circus, he never had a chance
   The judge made Rubin's witnesses drunkards from the slums
   To the white folks who watched he was a revolutionary bum
   And to the black folks he was just a crazy nigger
   No one doubted that he pulled the trigger
   And though they could not produce the gun
   The D.A. said he was the one who did the deed
   And the all-white jury agreed

10. Rubin Carter was falsely tried
    The crime was murder "one," guess who testified?
    Bello and Bradley and they both baldly lied
    And the newspapers, they all went along for the ride
    How can the life of such a man
    Be in the palm of some fool's hand?
    To see him obviously framed
    Couldn't help but make me feel ashamed to live in a land
    Where justice is a game

11. Now all the criminals in their coats and their ties
    Are free to drink martinis and watch the sun rise
    While Rubin sits like Buddha in a ten-foot cell
    An innocent man in a living hell
    That's the story of the Hurricane
    But it won't be over till they clear his name
    And give him back the time he's done
    Put in a prison cell, but one time he could-a been
    The champion of the world.

IT AIN'T ME BABE

Words and Music by
BOB DYLAN

Moderately fast

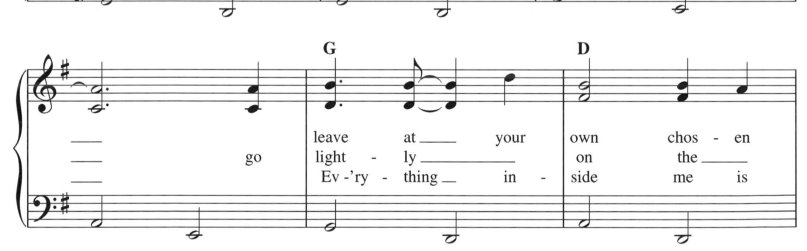

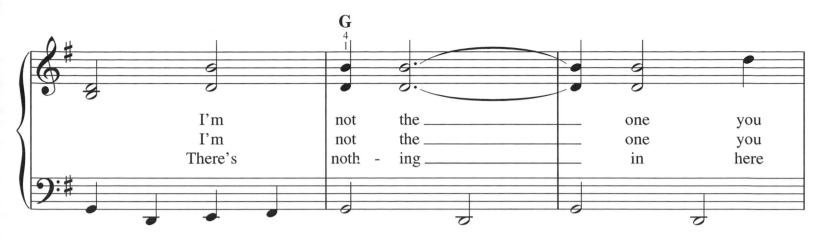

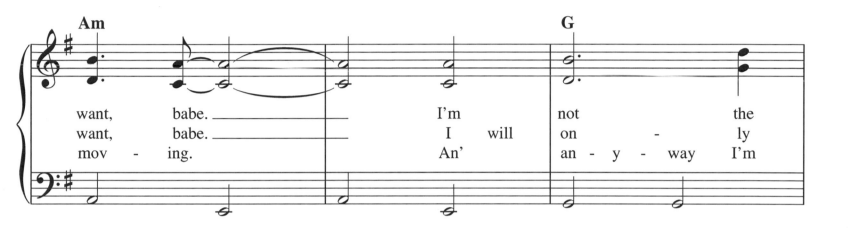

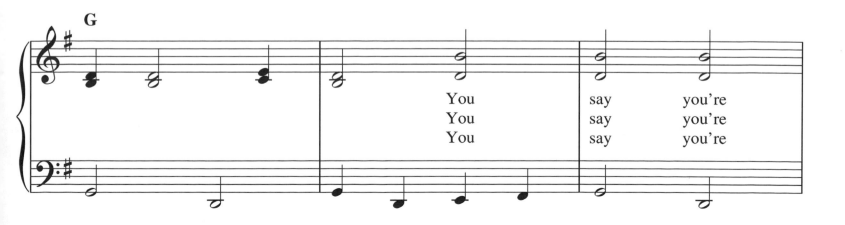

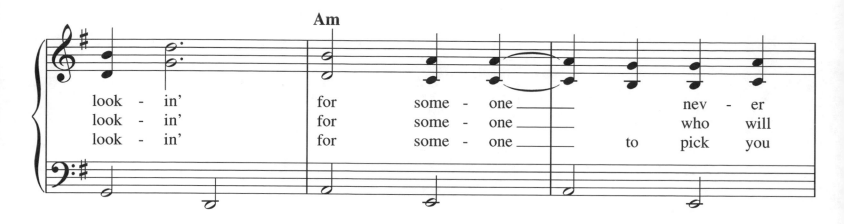

look - in'   for   some - one _____   nev - er
look - in'   for   some - one _____   who will
look - in'   for   some - one _____   to pick you

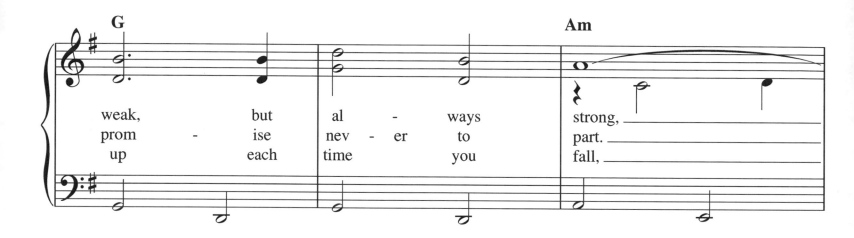

weak,   but   al   -   ways   strong, _____
prom   -   ise   nev - er   to   part. _____
up   each   time   you   fall, _____

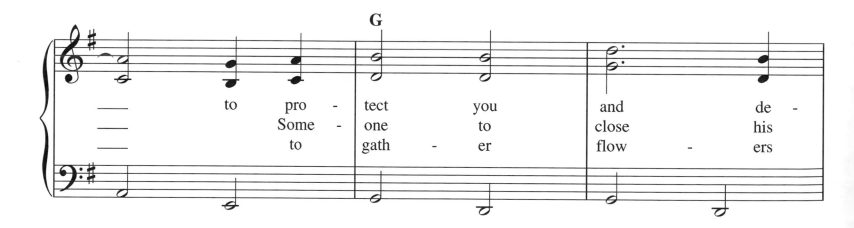

_____   to pro - tect   you   and   de -
_____   Some - one   to   gath - er   close   his
_____   to   gath - er   flow - ers

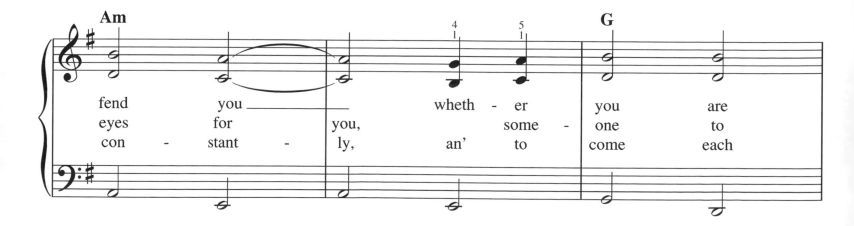

fend   you _____   wheth - er   you   are
eyes   for   you,   some - one   to
con - stant - ly,   an' to   come   each

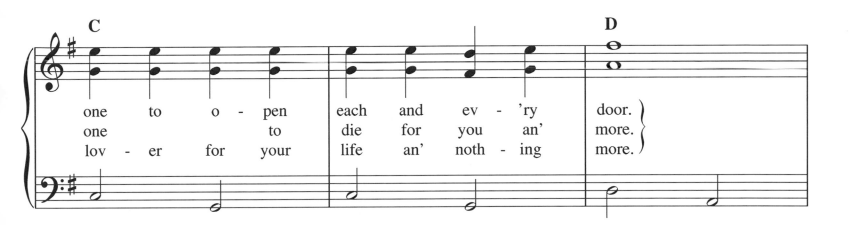

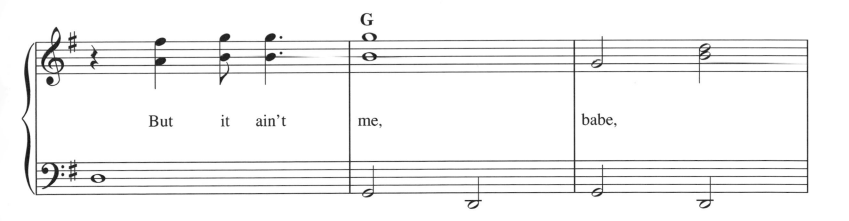

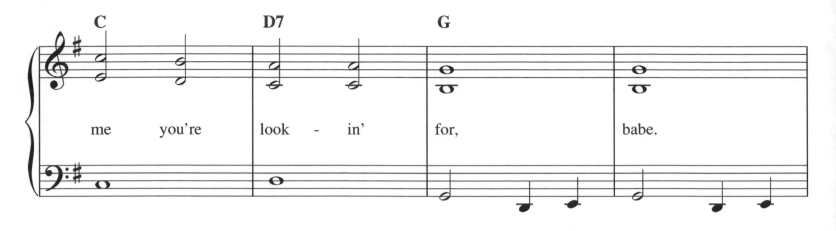

me you're look - in' for, babe.

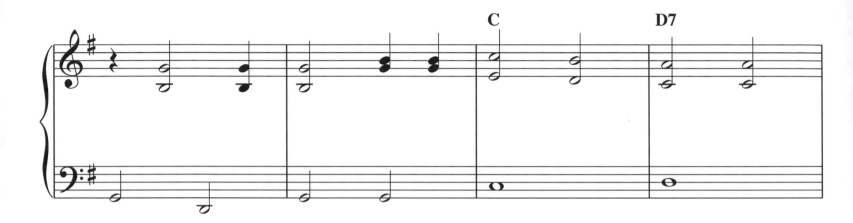

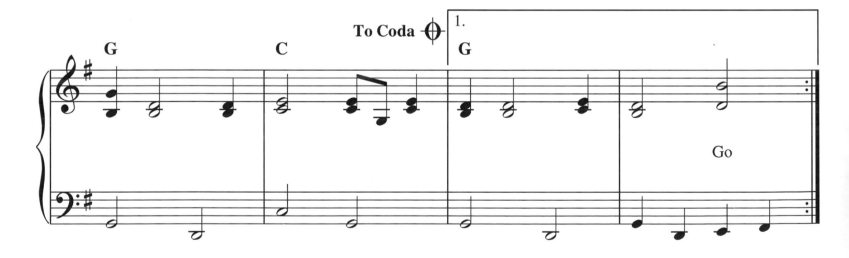

To Coda ⊕ 1.

Go

2.

D.S. al Coda

Go

CODA ⊕

rit.

LAY LADY LAY

Words and Music by
BOB DYLAN

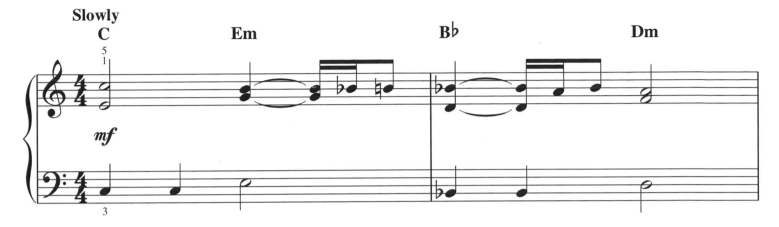

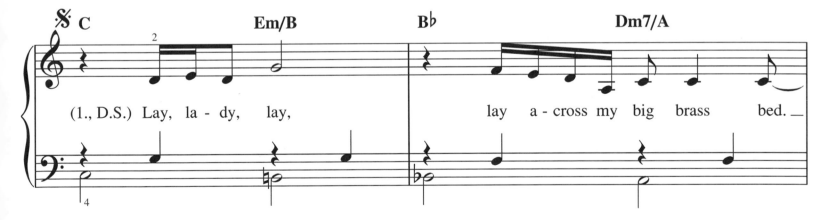

(1., D.S.) Lay, la-dy, lay, lay a-cross my big brass bed.

(1.) Lay, la-dy, lay,
(D.S.) Stay, la-dy, stay,

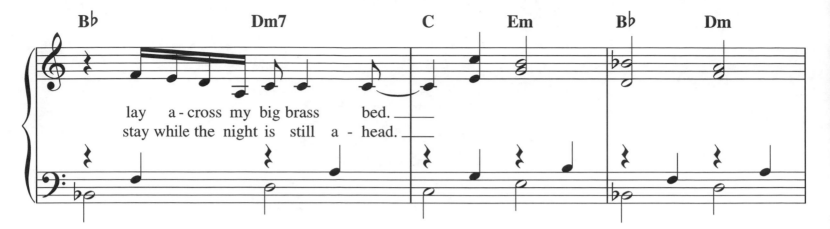

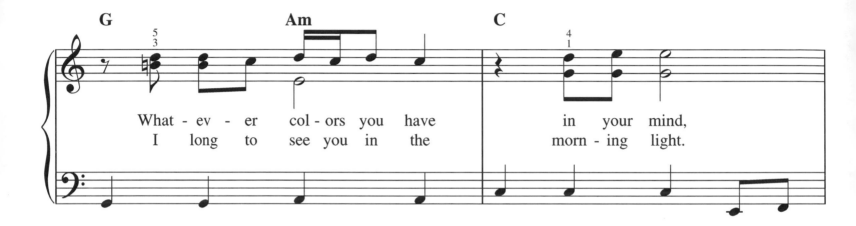

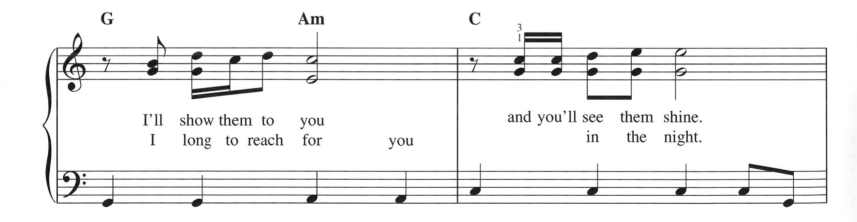

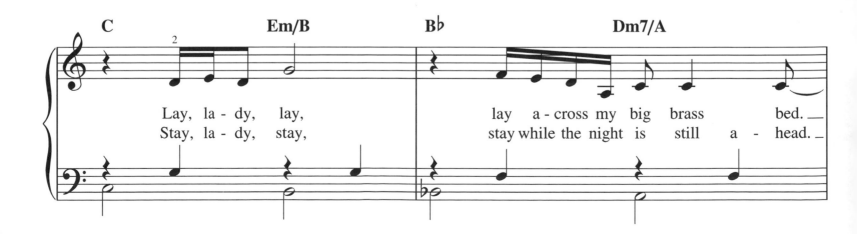

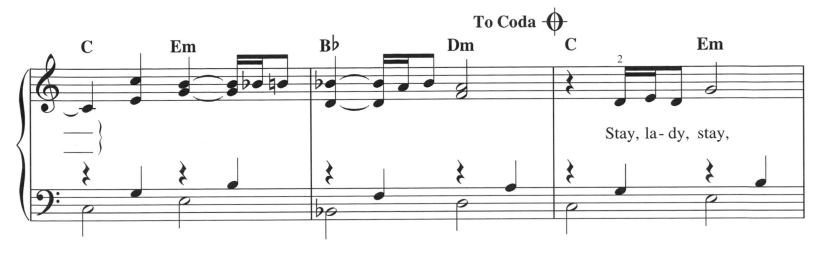

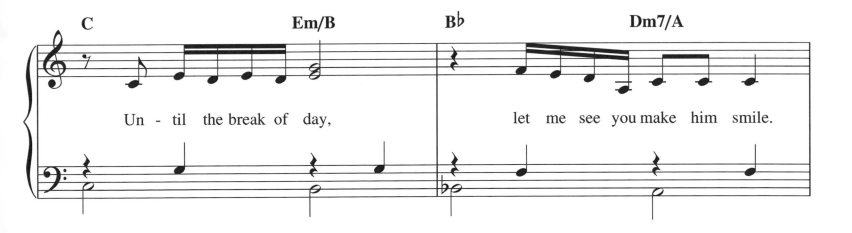

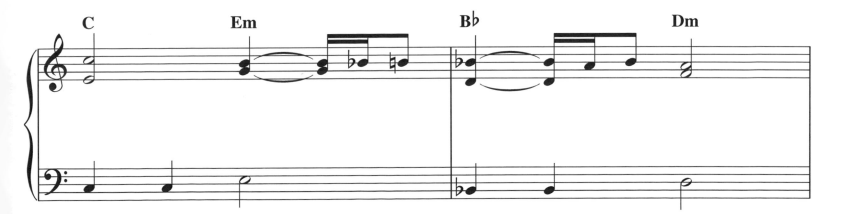

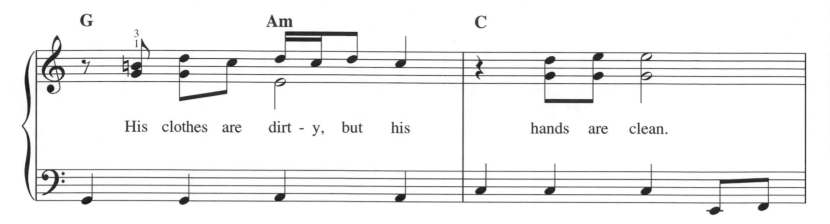

His clothes are dirt - y, but his hands are clean.

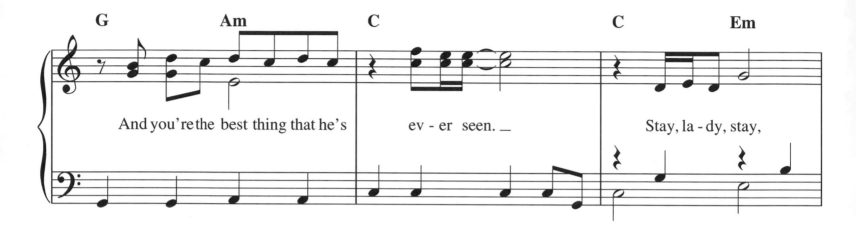

And you're the best thing that he's ev - er seen. ___ Stay, la - dy, stay,

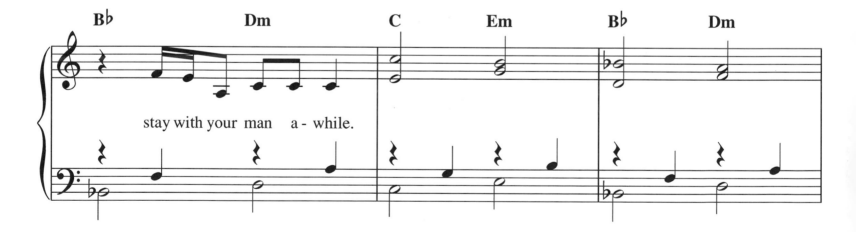

stay with your man a - while.

Why wait an - y long - er for ___ the world to be - gin? ___

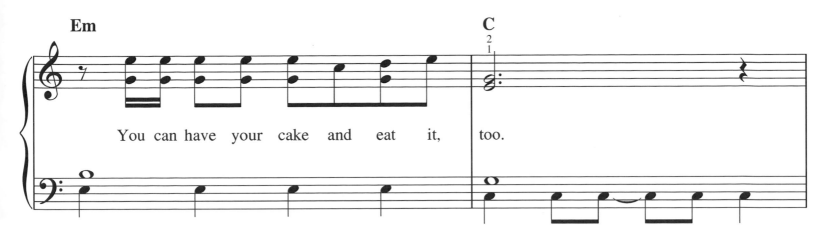

You can have your cake and eat it, too.

Why wait an-y long-er for the one you love ___ when he's

D.S. al Coda

stand - ing ___ in front of you? ___

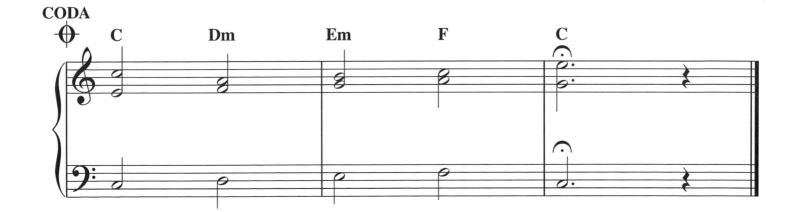

CODA

KNOCKIN' ON HEAVEN'S DOOR

Words and Music by
BOB DYLAN

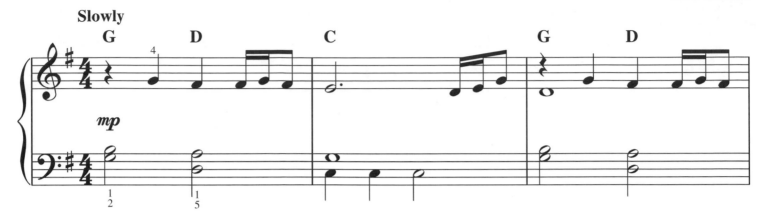

Ma-ma, take this badge off of me. _____
Ma-ma, put my guns on the ground. _____

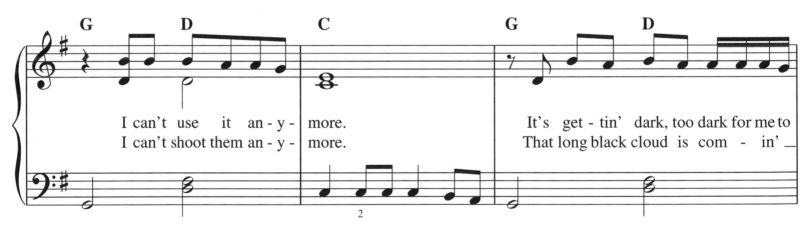

I can't use it an-y- more.
I can't shoot them an-y- more.

It's get-tin' dark, too dark for me to
That long black cloud is com - in'

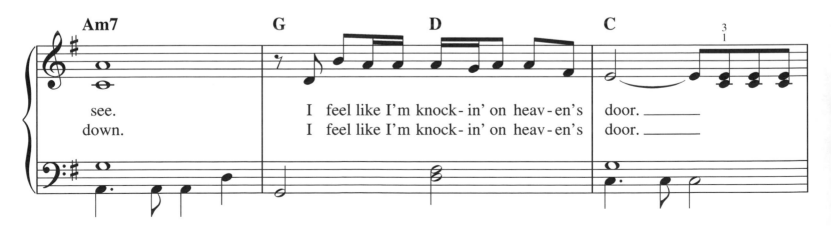

see.
down.

I feel like I'm knock-in' on heav-en's door. _____
I feel like I'm knock-in' on heav-en's door. _____

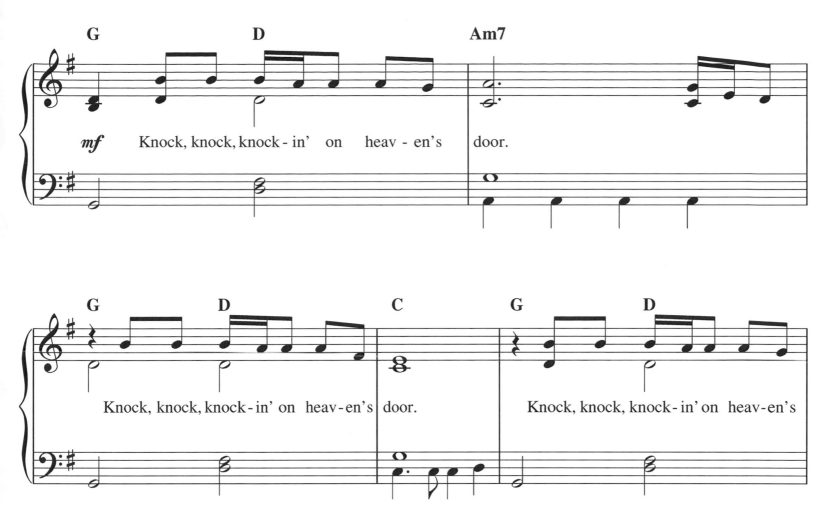

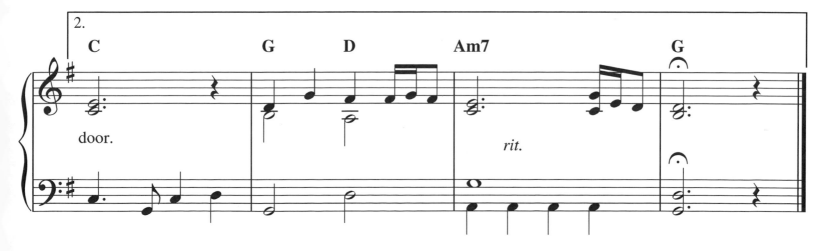

LIKE A ROLLING STONE

Words and Music by
BOB DYLAN

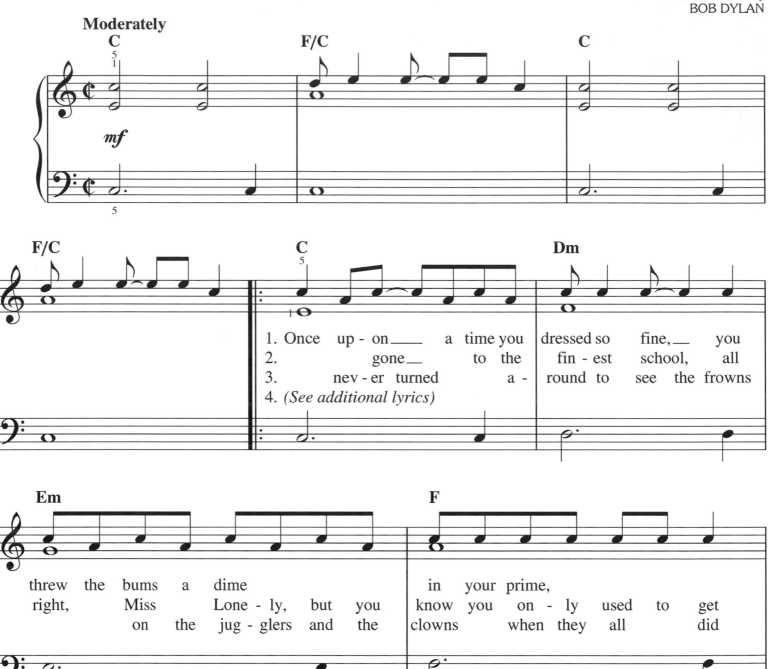

Moderately

1. Once up - on___ a time you dressed so fine,___ you threw the bums a dime in your prime, did - n't you?
2. ___ gone___ to the fin - est school, all right, Miss Lone - ly, but you know you on - ly used to juiced in it.
3. ___ nev - er turned a - round to see the frowns on the jug - glers and the clowns when they all did tricks for you.
4. *(See additional lyrics)*

C

Peo - ple'd call, say,___
And no - bod - y has ev - er taught you how
You nev - er___ un - der - stood that it

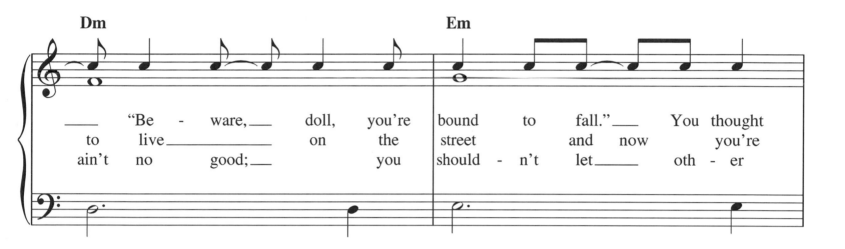

Dm   Em

___ "Be - ware,___ doll, you're bound to fall."___ You thought
to live___ on the street and now you're
ain't no good;___ you should - n't let___ oth - er

F   G

they were all
gon - na have to get
peo - ple get your

kid - din' you.
used to it.
kicks for you.

F

(3.) You used to ride on the chrome

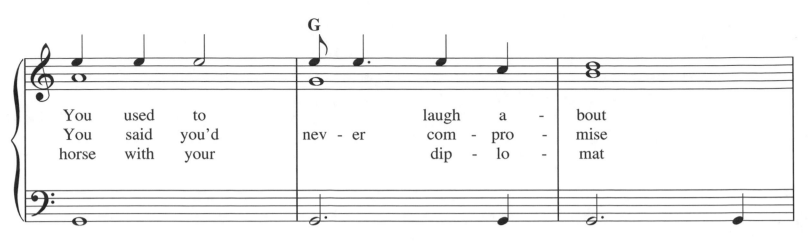

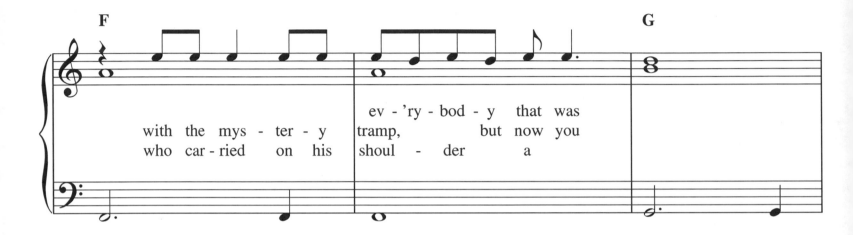

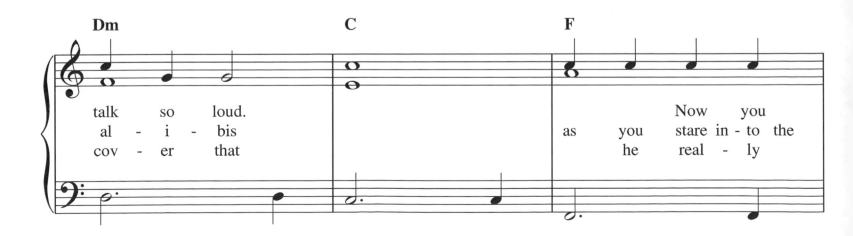

Em ... **Dm** ... **C**

don't | seem so proud | a -
vac - uum | of his eyes | and
was - n't | where it's at |

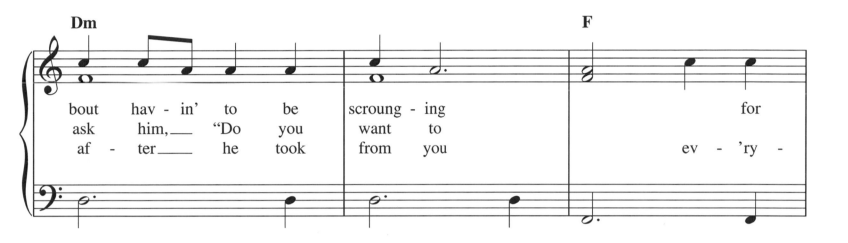

Dm ... **F**

bout hav - in' to be | scroung - ing | for
ask him,___ "Do you | want to |
af - ter___ he took | from you | ev - 'ry -

G

your next | meal.____
make a | deal?"_____
thing he could | steal?_____

Chorus

... **C**

How does it____ feel?____
(2.-4.) How does it____ feel?____

32

like a roll - ing stone?____

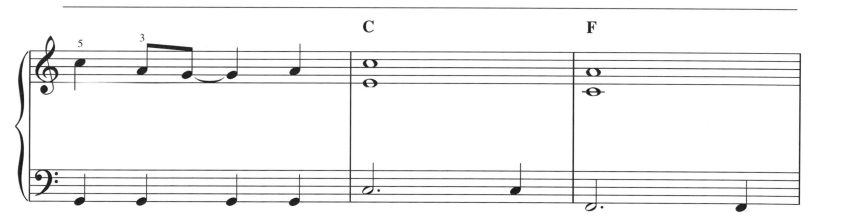

(2.) Oh, you've

34

like a com - plete un - known,

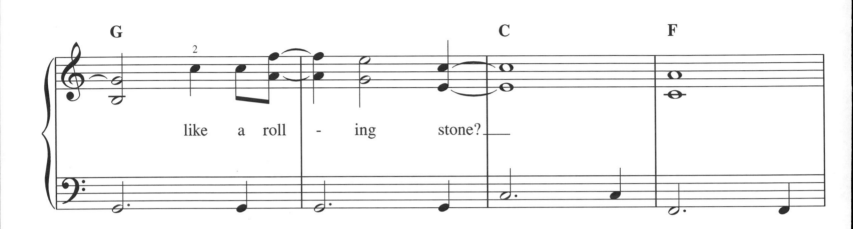

like a roll - ing stone?

(3.) Oh, you

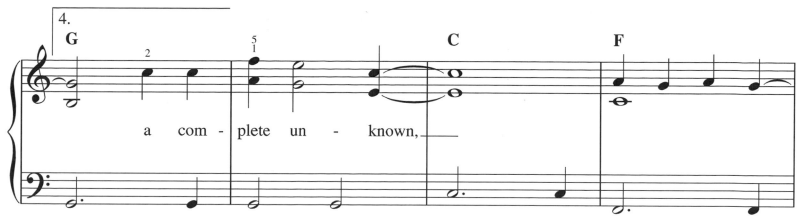

a com-plete un - known,

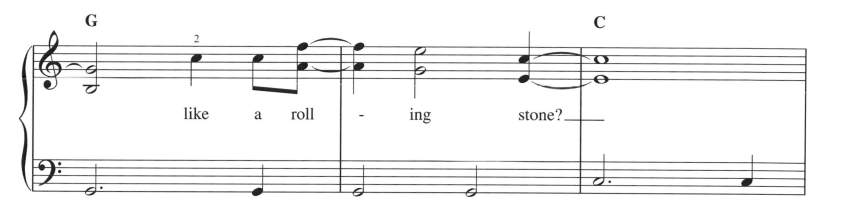

like a roll - ing stone?

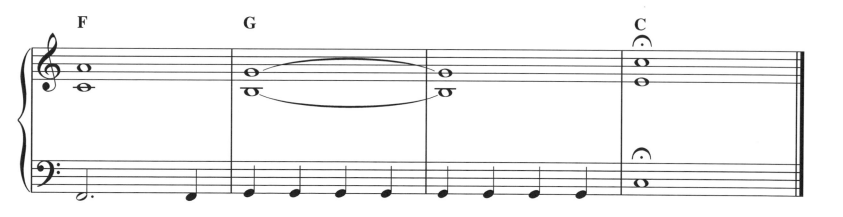

Additional Lyrics

4. Princess on the steeple and all the pretty people
   They're all drinkin', thinkin' that they got it made.
   Exchanging all kinds of precious gifts and things.
   But you'd better lift your diamond ring,
   You'd better pawn it, babe.
   You used to be so amused
   At Napoleon in rags and the language that he used.
   Go to him now, he calls you, you can't refuse.
   When you got nothing, you got nothing to lose.
   You're invisible now, you got no secrets to conceal.
   Chorus

MR. TAMBOURINE MAN

Words and Music by
BOB DYLAN

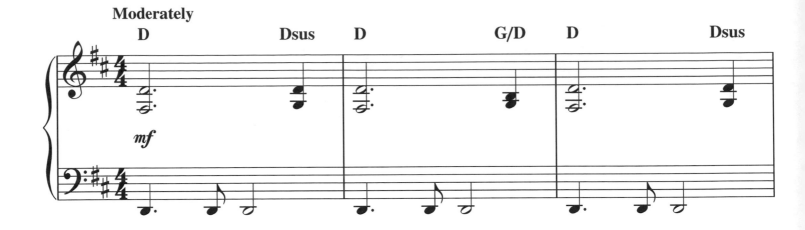

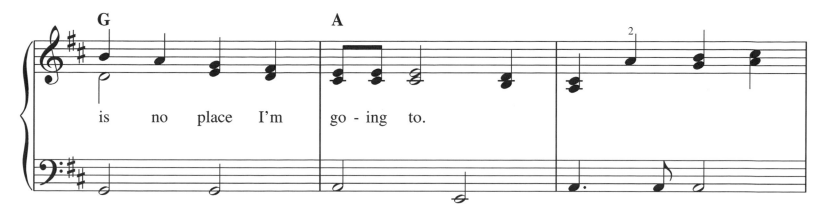

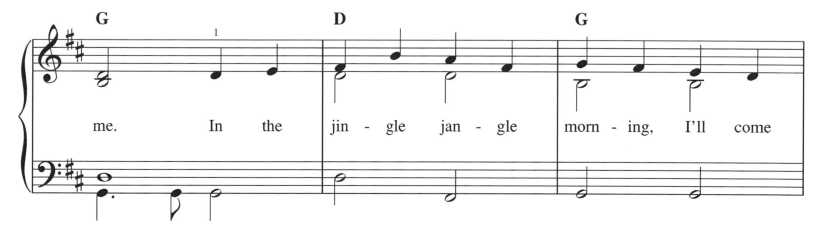

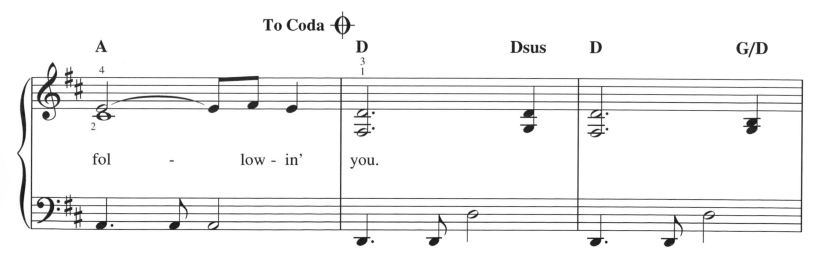

1. Though I know that eve - nin's
2.-4. *(See additional lyrics)*

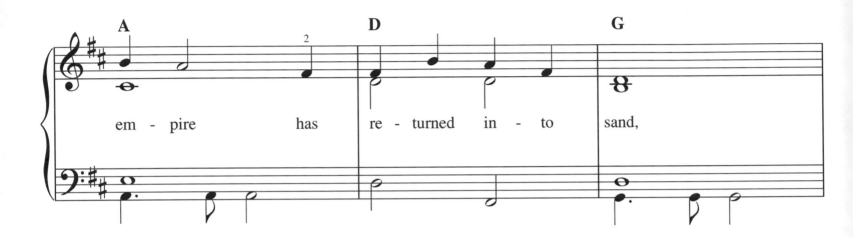

em - pire has re - turned in - to sand,

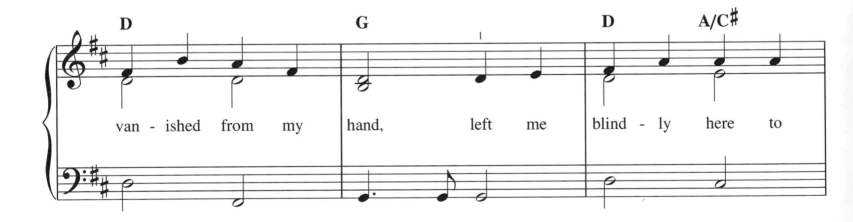

van - ished from my hand, left me blind - ly here to

stand but still not sleep - ing! ___ My

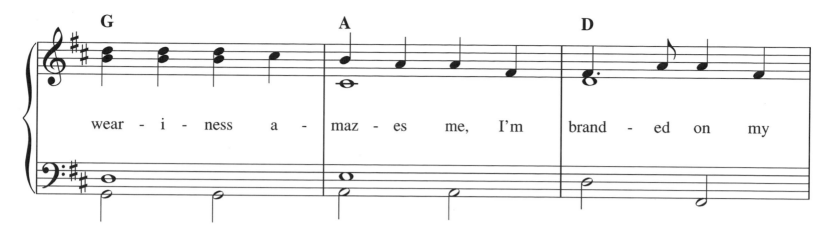

wear - i - ness a - maz - es me, I'm brand - ed on my

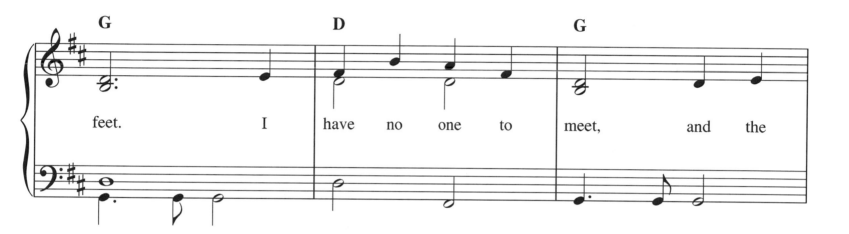

feet. I have no one to meet, and the

an - cient emp - ty street's too dead for dream - in'. _____

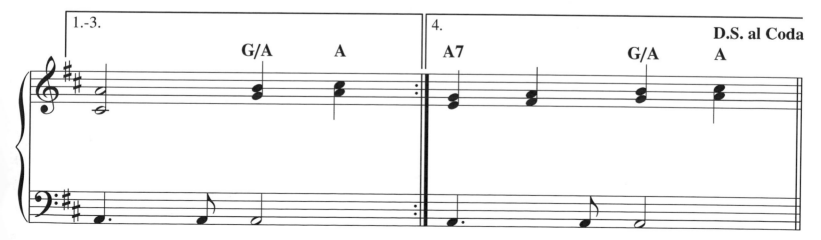

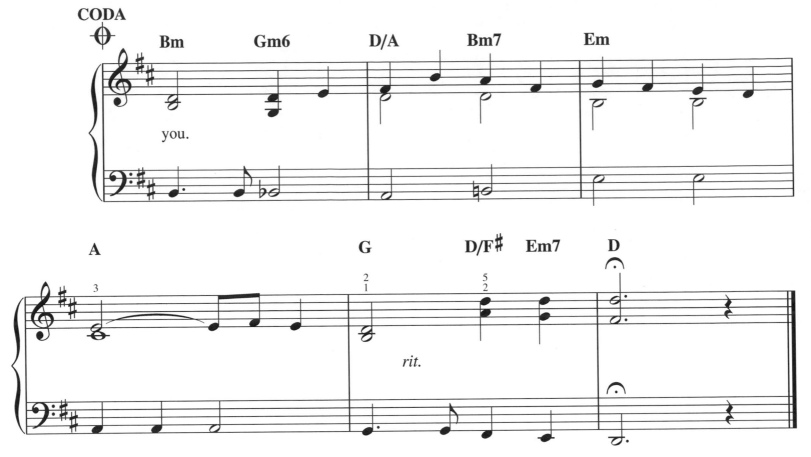

Additional Lyrics

2. Take me on a trip upon your magic swirlin' ship
   My senses have been stripped, my hands can't feel to grip
   My toes too numb to step,
   Wait only for my boot heels to be wanderin'
   I'm ready to go anywhere, I'm ready for to fade
   Into my own parade, cast your dancing spell my way
   I promise to go under it

3. Though you might hear laughin', spinnin', swingin' madly across the sun
   It's not aimed at anyone, it's just escapin' on the run
   And but for the sky there are no fences facin'
   And if you hear vague traces of skippin' reels of rhyme
   To your tambourine in time, it's just a ragged clown behind
   I wouldn't pay it any mind,
   It's just a shadow you're seein' that he's chasing

4. Then take me disappearin' through the smoke rings of my mind
   Down the foggy ruins of time, far past the frozen leaves
   The haunted, frightened trees, out to the windy beach
   Far from the twisted reach of crazy sorrow
   Yes, to dance beneath the diamond sky with one hand waving free
   Silhouetted by the sea, circled by the circus sands
   With all memory and fate driven deep beneath the waves
   Let me forget about today until tomorrow

RAINY DAY WOMEN #12 & 35

Words and Music by
BOB DYLAN

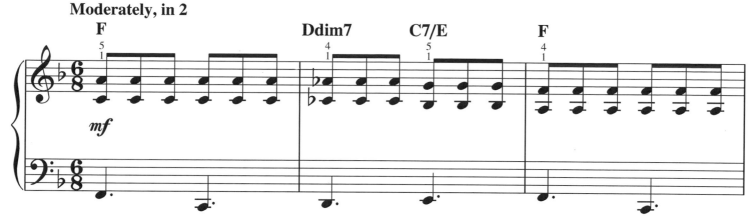

1. Well, they'll stone ya when you're try - ing to be so
2.-5. *(See additional lyrics)*

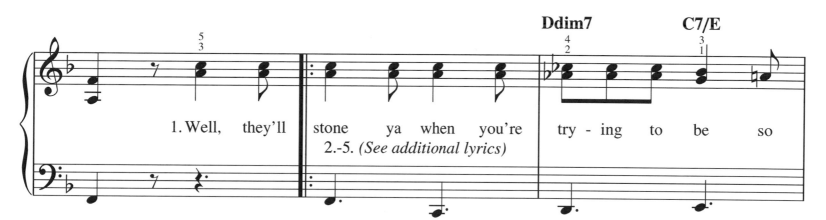

good. _____ They'll stone ya just a -

like they said they would. _____ They'll

stone ya when you're try - in' to go home. _____

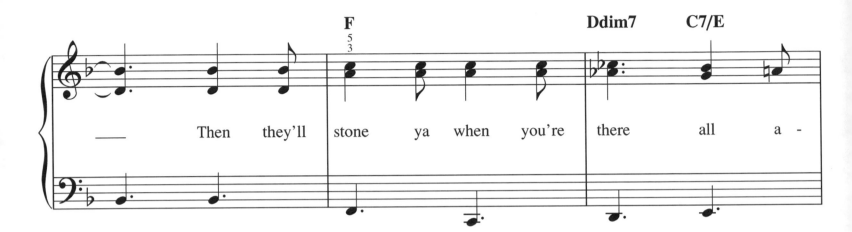

_____ Then they'll stone ya when you're there all a -

lone. _____ But I would not _____ feel _____

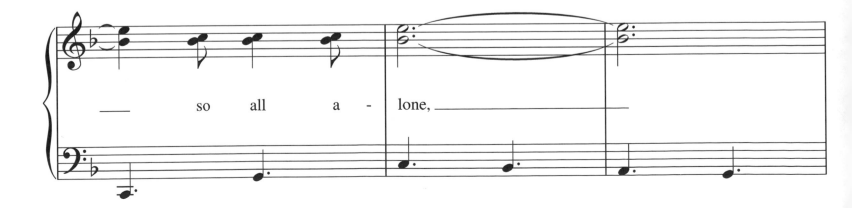

_____ so all a - lone, _____

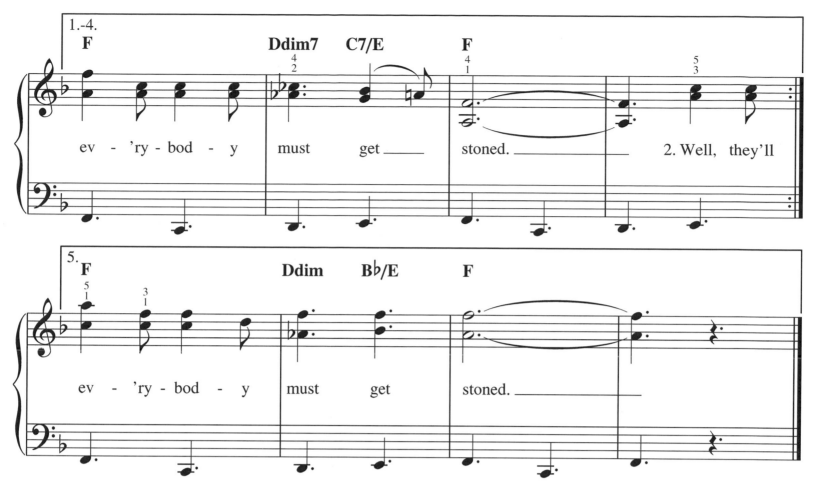

Additional Lyrics

2. Well, they'll stone ya when you're walkin' 'long the street.
   They'll stone ya when you're tryin' keep your seat.
   They'll stone ya when you're walkin' on the floor.
   They'll stone ya when you're walkin' to the door.
   But I would not feel so all alone,
   Everybody must get stoned.

3. They'll stone ya when you're at the breakfast table,
   They'll stone ya when you are young and able.
   They'll stone ya when you're tryin' to make a buck.
   They'll stone ya and then they'll say, "Good luck."
   Tell ya what, I would not feel so all alone,
   Everybody must get stoned.

4. Well, they'll stone you and say that it's the end.
   Then they'll stone you and then they'll come back again.
   They'll stone you when you're riding in your car.
   They'll stone you when you're playing your guitar.
   Yes, but I would not feel so all alone,
   Everybody must get stoned.

5. Well, they'll stone you when you walk all alone.
   They'll stone you when you are walking home.
   They'll stone you and then say you are brave.
   They'll stone you when you are set down in your grave.
   But I would not feel so all alone,
   Everybody must get stoned.

SHELTER FROM THE STORM

Words and Music by
BOB DYLAN

Moderately fast

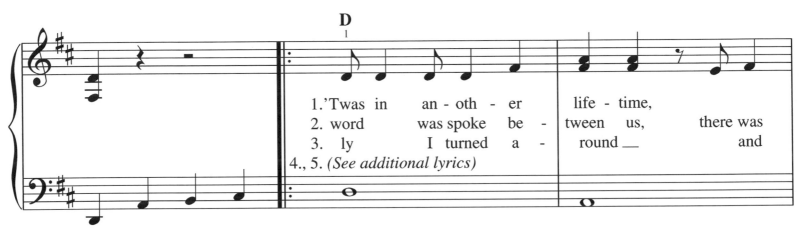

1.'Twas in an - oth - er life - time,
2. word was spoke be - tween us, there was
3. ly I turned a - round and
4., 5. *(See additional lyrics)*

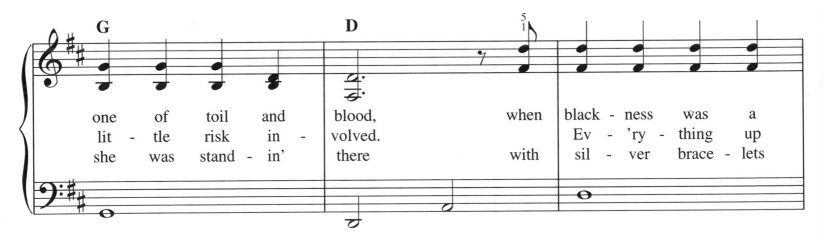

one of toil and blood, when black - ness was a
lit - tle risk in - volved. Ev - 'ry - thing up
she was stand - in' there with sil - ver brace - lets

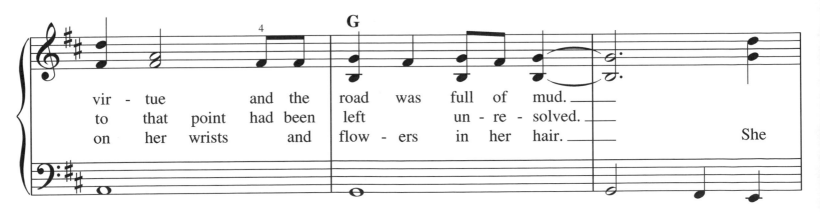

vir - tue and the road was full of mud.
to that point had been left un - re - solved.
on her wrists and flow - ers in her hair. She

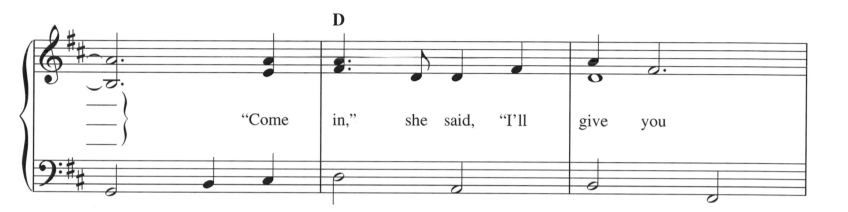

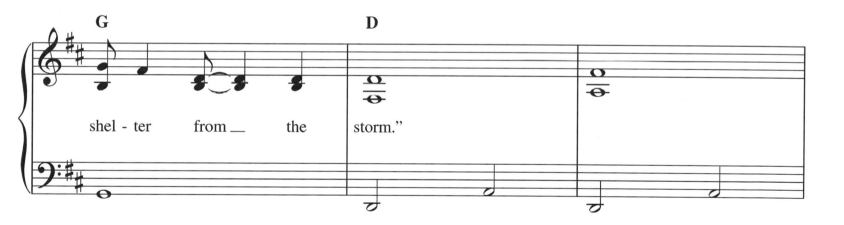

way a - gain,   you can   rest   as - sured   I'll
haus - tion,   bur - ied   in   the   hail,
tween us,   some - thin'   there's   been   lost.   I

al - ways   do   my   best   for   her,   on   that   I   give   my
poi - soned   in   the   bush - es   an'   blown out   on   the
took   too   much   for   grant - ed,   got   my   sig - nals

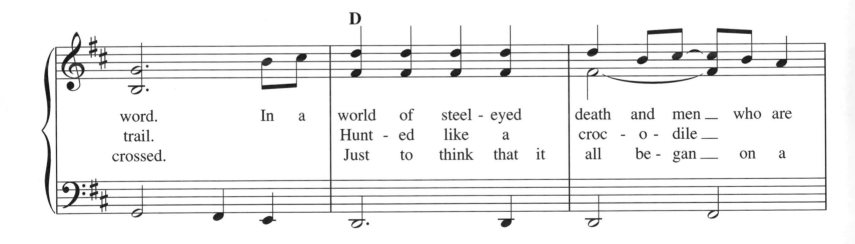

word.   In   a   world   of   steel - eyed   death   and   men __ who are
trail.   Hunt - ed   like   a   croc - o - dile __
crossed.   Just   to   think   that   it   all   be - gan __ on a

fight - ing   to   be   warm, ⎫
rav - aged   in   the   corn, ⎬   "Come   in,"   she said,   "I'll
long   for - got - ten   morn, ⎭

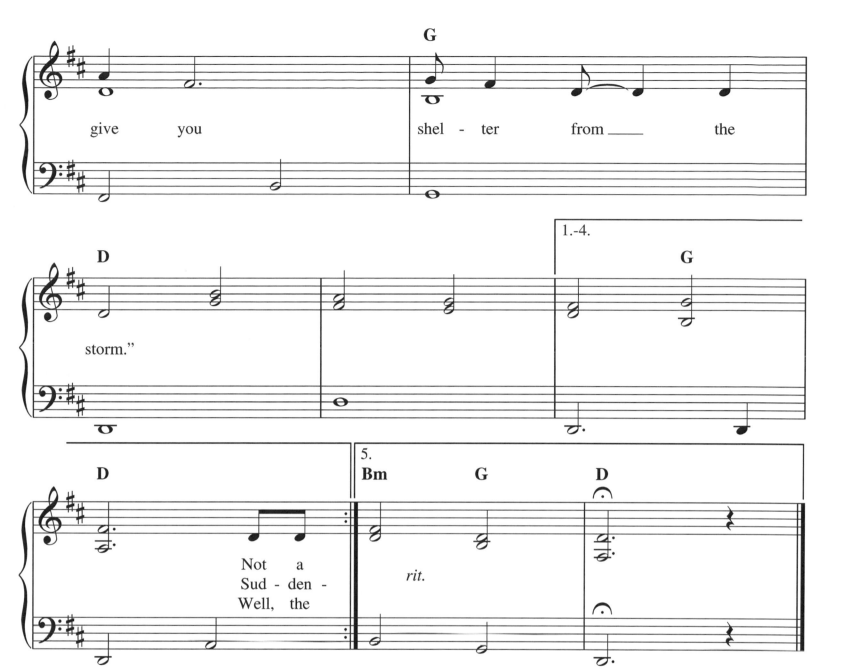

Additional Lyrics

4. Well, the deputy walks on hard nails
   And the preacher rides a mount
   But nothing really matters much
   It's doom alone that counts.
   And the one-eyed undertaker,
   He blows a futile horn
   "Come in," she said, "I'll give you
   Shelter from the storm."

   I've heard newborn babies wailin'
   Like a mornin' dove
   And old men with broken teeth
   Stranded without love.
   Do I understand your question, man,
   Is it hopeless and forlorn?
   "Come in," she said, "I'll give you
   Shelter from the storm."

5. In a little hilltop village
   They gambled for my clothes
   I bargained for salvation
   An' they gave me a lethal dose.
   I offered up my innocence
   And got repaid with scorn
   "Come in," she said, "I'll give you
   Shelter from the storm."

   Well, I'm livin' in a foreign country
   But I'm bound to cross the line
   Beauty walks a razor's edge,
   Someday I'll make it mine.
   If I could only turn back the clock
   To when God and her were born
   "Come in," she said, "I'll give you
   Shelter from the storm."

TANGLED UP IN BLUE

Words and Music by
BOB DYLAN

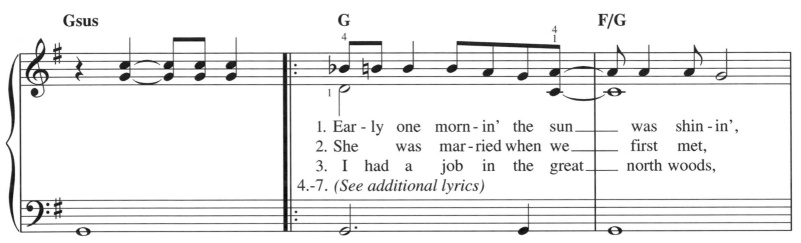

1. Ear - ly one morn - in' the sun___ was shin - in',
2. She was mar - ried when we___ first met,
3. I had a job in the great___ north woods,
4.-7. *(See additional lyrics)*

I was lay - in' in bed___
soon to be di - vorced.___
work - in' as a cook for a spell.___ But I

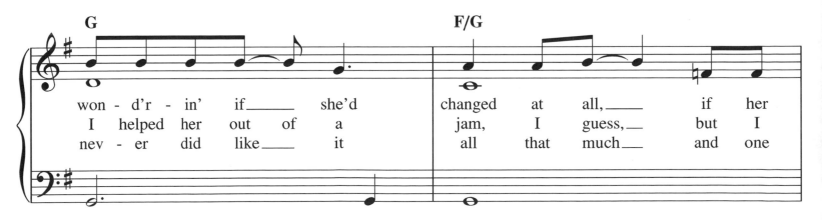

won - d'r - in' if___ she'd
I helped her out of a
nev - er did like___ it

changed at all,___ if her
jam, I guess,___ but I
all that much___ and one

49

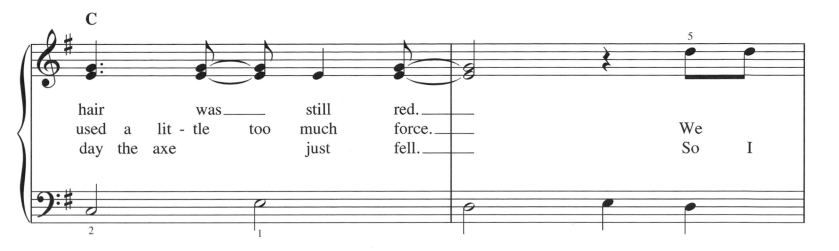

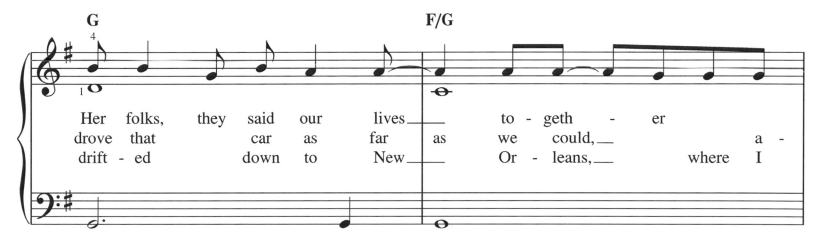

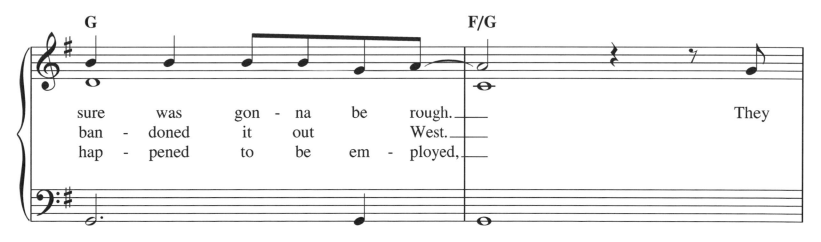

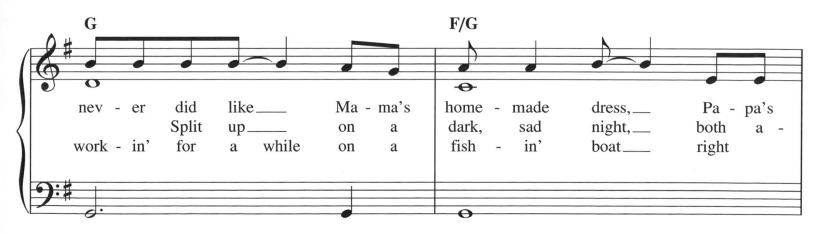

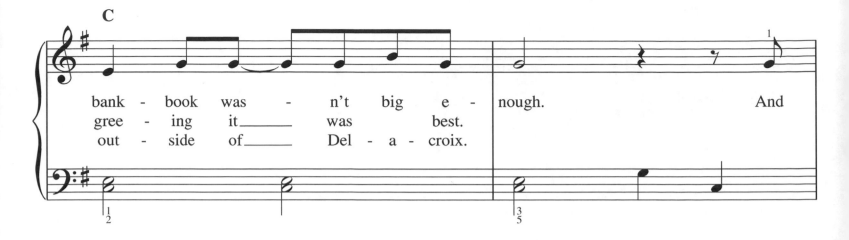

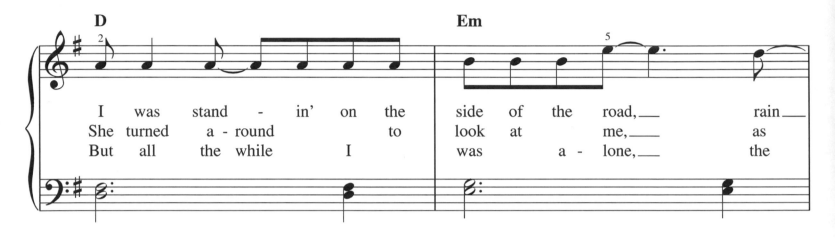

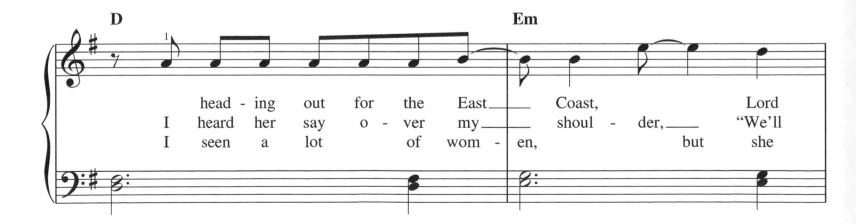

knows I've paid some dues _____ gettin' through. _____
meet a - gain some - day _____ on the av - e - nue." _____
nev - er es - caped my mind, _____ and I just grew _____

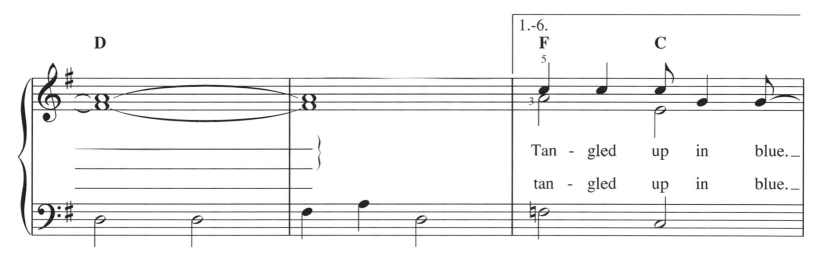

1.-6.

Tan - gled up in blue. _____
tan - gled up in blue. _____

Additional Lyrics

4. She was workin' in a topless place
   And I stopped in for a beer.
   I just kept lookin' at the side of her face
   In the spotlight so clear.
   And later on when the crowd thinned out
   I's just about to do the same.
   She was standing there in back of my chair,
   Said to me, "Don't I know your name?"
   I muttered something underneath my breath.
   She studied the lines on my face.
   I must admit I felt a little uneasy
   When she bent down to tie the laces of my shoe,
   Tangled up in blue.

5. She lit a burner on the stove
   And offered me a pipe.
   "I thought you'd never say hello," she said.
   "You look like the silent type."
   Then she opened up a book of poems
   And handed it to me,
   Written by an Italian poet
   From the thirteenth century.
   And every one of them words rang true
   And glowed like burnin' coal,
   Pourin' off of every page
   Like it was written in my soul, from me to you,
   Tangled up in blue.

6. I lived with them on Montague Street
   In a basement down the stairs.
   There was music in the cafés at night
   And revolution in the air.
   Then he started into dealing with slaves
   And something inside of him died.
   She had to sell everything she owned
   And froze up inside.
   And when finally the bottom fell out
   I became withdrawn.
   The only thing I knew how to do
   Was to keep on keepin' on, like a bird that flew
   Tangled up in blue.

7. So now I'm goin' back again.
   I got to get to her somehow.
   All the people we used to know,
   They're an illusion to me now.
   Some are mathematicians,
   Some are carpenters' wives.
   Don't know how it all got started,
   I don't know what they're doin' with their lives.
   But me, I'm still on the road
   Headin' for another joint.
   We always did feel the same,
   We just saw it from a different point of view,
   Tangled up in blue.

THE TIMES THEY ARE A-CHANGIN'

Words and Music by
BOB DYLAN

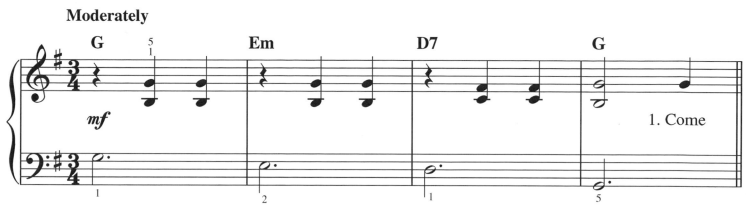

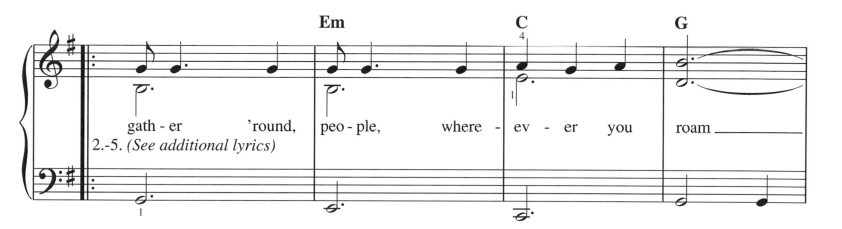

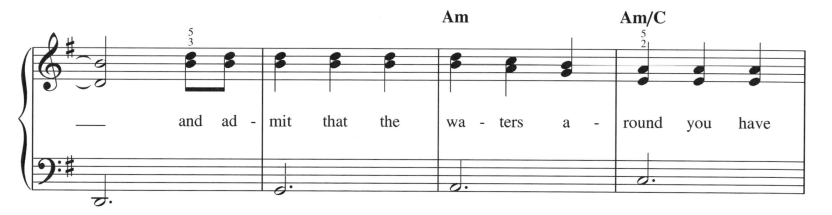

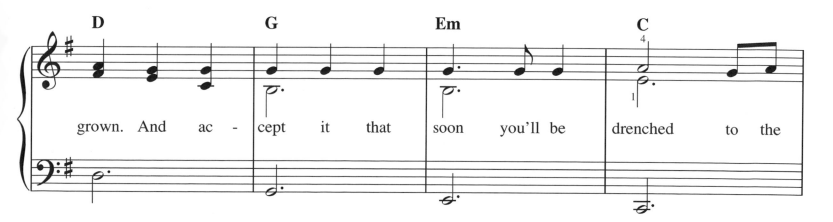

bone. _____ If your time to you is worth

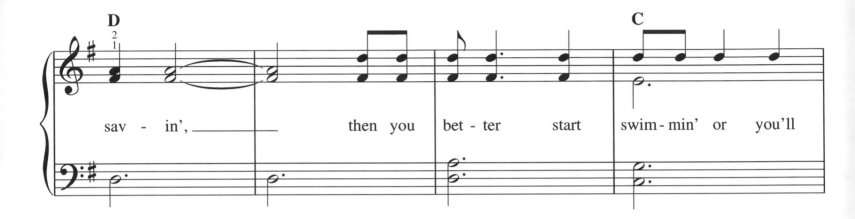

sav - in', _____ then you bet - ter start swim-min' or you'll

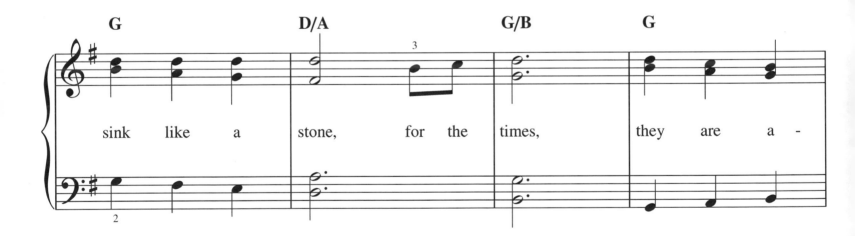

sink like a stone, for the times, they are a -

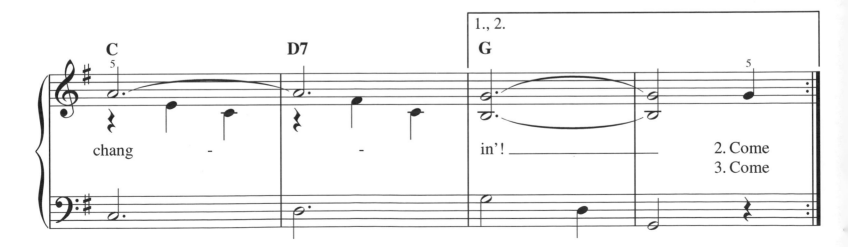

chang - - in'! _____ 2. Come
3. Come

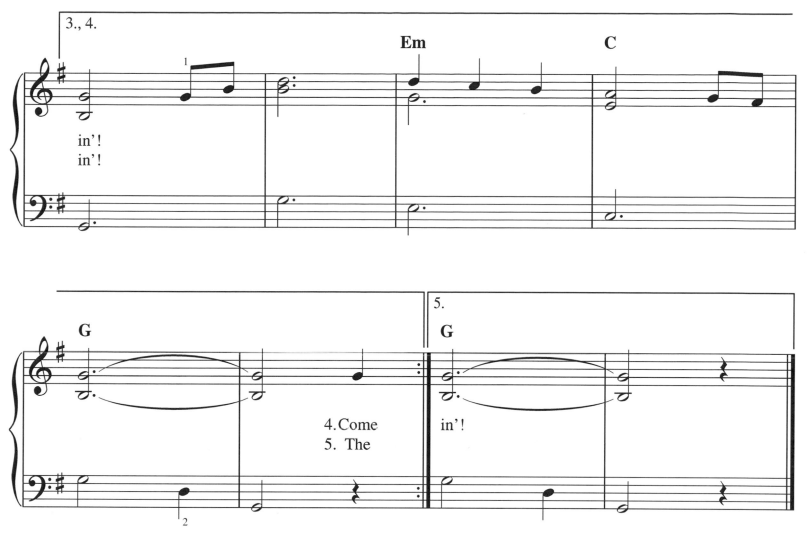

Additional Lyrics

2. Come writers and critics
   Who prophesize with your pen
   And keep your eyes wide
   The chance won't come again.
   And don't speak too soon
   For the wheel's still in spin,
   And there's no tellin' who that it's namin'
   For the loser now will be later to win.
   For the times, they are a-changin'!

3. Come senators, congressmen
   Please heed the call
   Don't stand in the doorway
   Don't block up the hall.
   For he that gets hurt
   Will be he who has stalled,
   There's a battle outside and it's ragin'.
   It'll soon shake your windows
   and rattle your walls,
   For the times, they are a-changin'!

4. Come mothers and fathers
   Throughout the land
   And don't criticize
   What you can't understand.
   Your sons and your daughters
   Are beyond your command,
   Your old road is rapidly agin'.
   Please get out of the new one
   if you can't lend your hand,
   For the times, they are a-changin'!

5. The line is drawn
   The curse is cast
   The slow one now
   Will later be fast.
   As the present now
   Will later be past.
   The order is rapidly fadin'.
   And the first one now will later be last,
   For the times, they are a-changin'!